# Longman Atlas of World Issues

Selected by
**Robert J. Art**
*Brandeis University*

PEARSON
Longman

New York  Boston  San Francisco
London  Toronto  Sydney  Tokyo  Singapore  Madrid
Mexico City  Munich  Paris  Cape Town  Hong Kong  Montreal

Acknowledgements:

Maps by Myriad Editions Ltd., from *Penguin Atlas of War and Peace,*
*Fourth Edition,* © 2003, *Penguin State of the World Atlas, Seventh Edition*
© 2003, *Penguin Atlas of Media and Information* (2001), and *Penguin*
*Atlas of Human Sexual Behavior* (2000). Used by permission of Penguin
Group, USA, Inc.

*Longman Atlas of World Issues*

Copyright ©2005 Pearson Education

ISBN: 0-321-22465-5

9  10-RRD-O-10 09

# Table of Contents

# PREFACE

Today, the world remains divided into geographically distinct states, and at last count, there were 192 of them. A simple map of the world would show their shape, size, and location on the globe. Such a rendering, however, would give only a rudimentary sense of how states differ and how they are similar, what goes on inside of them, the myriad ways in which they interact, and how transnational factors affect them. To give a full picture of what states look like and how they interact requires more than a simple rendering of state boundaries.

This volume is designed to give that picture. It contains twenty-one maps that present students with important facts, figures, and statistics – all in an easy to read pictorial format – about some of the most important factors that define states and their interactions with one another. Clearly, such a small volume as this cannot be exhaustive; nonetheless, the maps contained here do present a wide range of information about the world today and the peoples and the states that comprise it.

The maps are divided into four parts: general contours of the world, dimensions of violent conflict, international political economy, and human problems. These maps cover subjects that range from the state of human rights to climate change. Taken together, these twenty-one maps show a world of tremendous diversity, marred by serious inequalities, yet also marked by considerable progress. War has not been banished, refugees are far too numerous and poorly taken care of, drugs continue to take their toll, and women have not achieved full equality. And yet, women have made considerable progress in gaining their rights; trade has increased and remains an important engine of growth, especially for Third World states; and human rights and democracy continue to advance.

These maps are useful not only for introductory courses in international relations, but also for courses in comparative politics, global studies, and any others that deal with the world as a whole.

---Robert J. Art, Brandeis University

A major feature of the end of the 20th century was the global transition to democracy. It brought many benefits in terms of freedom, the rule of law, and peace. Democratic states tend not to go to war with each other and though all states that can formally call themselves democratic are about as likely to experience civil war as all states that are straightforward dictatorships, the well established democracies are far more stable than dictatorships. However, while democracy is relatively safe from war, the path to it is full of dangers. At the turn of the millennium:

• Of established democracies, 12 percent were involved in civil war.

• Of one party dictatorships, 45 percent were involved in civil war.

• Of states with a transitional or uncertain democracy, 30 percent were involved in civil war.

War in transitional democracies was a major factor in the increase in armed conflict during the 1990s, especially in the former USSR and ex-Yugoslavia. When the rules of the game are not clear, not accepted by all parties, and not well established, political rivalries are pursued by any means possible. Electoral defeat – or its expectation – may be the spur to war.

From *The Penguin Atlas of War and Peace* (ISBN 0142002941)
Copyright © Myriad Editions / www.MyriadEditions.com

# Political Systems

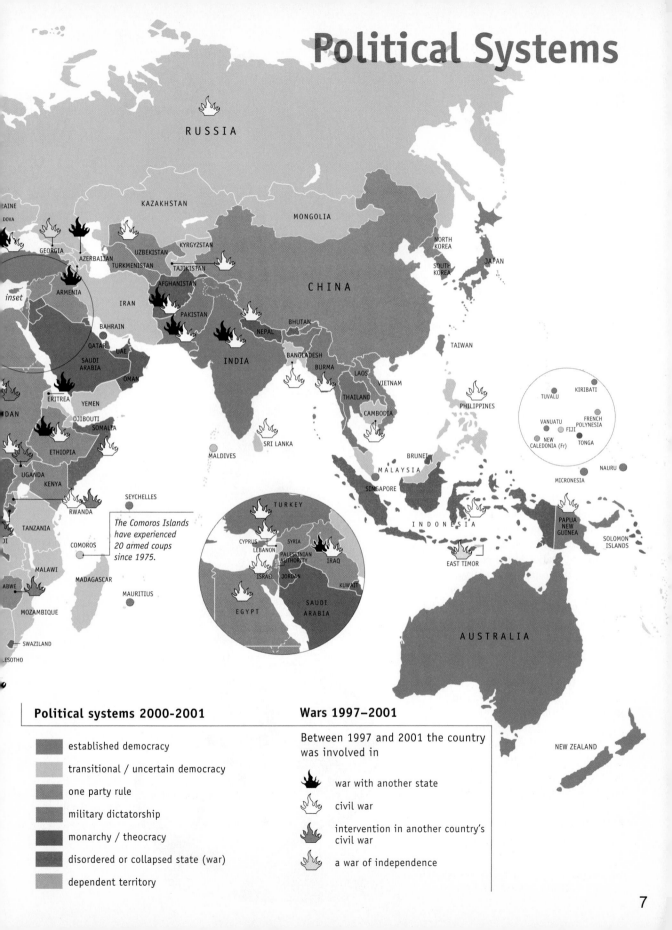

RUSSIA

KAZAKHSTAN

MONGOLIA

NORTH KOREA

SOUTH KOREA

JAPAN

UKRAINE

MOLDOVA

GEORGIA

AZERBAIJAN

UZBEKISTAN

TURKMENISTAN

TAJIKISTAN

KYRGYZSTAN

*inset*

ARMENIA

IRAN

AFGHANISTAN

PAKISTAN

CHINA

BAHRAIN

QATAR

UAE

SAUDI ARABIA

OMAN

NEPAL

BHUTAN

INDIA

BANGLADESH

BURMA

TAIWAN

ERITREA

YEMEN

DJIBOUTI

SOMALIA

SUDAN

ETHIOPIA

LAOS

VIETNAM

THAILAND

CAMBODIA

PHILIPPINES

TUVALU

KIRIBATI

VANUATU

FRENCH POLYNESIA

NEW CALEDONIA (Fr)

FIJI

TONGA

UGANDA

KENYA

RWANDA

SEYCHELLES

MALDIVES

SRI LANKA

BRUNEI

MALAYSIA

SINGAPORE

MICRONESIA

NAURU

TANZANIA

BURUNDI

COMOROS

The Comoros Islands have experienced 20 armed coups since 1975.

MALAWI

MADAGASCAR

MAURITIUS

INDONESIA

PAPUA NEW GUINEA

SOLOMON ISLANDS

EAST TIMOR

ZIMBABWE

MOZAMBIQUE

TURKEY

CYPRUS

LEBANON

SYRIA

PALESTINIAN AUTHORITY

ISRAEL

JORDAN

IRAQ

KUWAIT

SWAZILAND

LESOTHO

EGYPT

SAUDI ARABIA

AUSTRALIA

NEW ZEALAND

## Political systems 2000-2001

- established democracy
- transitional / uncertain democracy
- one party rule
- military dictatorship
- monarchy / theocracy
- disordered or collapsed state (war)
- dependent territory

## Wars 1997–2001

Between 1997 and 2001 the country was involved in

- war with another state
- civil war
- intervention in another country's civil war
- a war of independence

# International organizations
*2002*

Members of:

**African Union**

**Association of Southeast Asian Nations (ASEAN)**

**Commonwealth of Independent States (CIS)**

**European Union (EU)** *2002*

**European Union new members** *projected 2004*

**League of Arab States**

**Free Trade Area of the Americas (FTAA)**

**other countries and territories**

Organization for Economic Cooperation and Development (OECD)

Organization of the Petroleum Exporting Countries (OPEC)

Asia Pacific Economic Cooperation (APEC)

The term "international community" is frequently and loosely used to try and express the idea of an international consensus for or against particular states or actions. It has become one of the clichés of international politics. But there is a degree of reality in the concept of an international community, along with the rhetoric. As states regulate their mutual affairs through treaties and agreements, so the scope of international law grows, and slowly its effectiveness is increasing too.

Within this international framework, states act together in groupings defined by region, by common strategic interest or – in the case of the G8 – simply by economic clout. In any group of states, it is the weaker ones that have the most interest in building a genuine community, and the strongest that have the most reservations.

**GDP of G8 countries**
Canada, France, Germany, Italy, Japan, Russia, UK, USA
**$21,136 million**

**67%**

**GDP of rest of world**
**$10,179 million**

**33%**

**World GDP**
**$31,315 million**

From *The Penguin State of the World Atlas* (ISBN 0142003182)
Copyright © Myriad Editions / www.MyriadEditions.com

# International Organizations

Many states belong to regional organizations through which, with varying degrees of success, they attempt to pursue their economic, political and strategic interests.

**NATO**
Members of North Atlantic Treaty Organization

2002

projected to join by May 2004

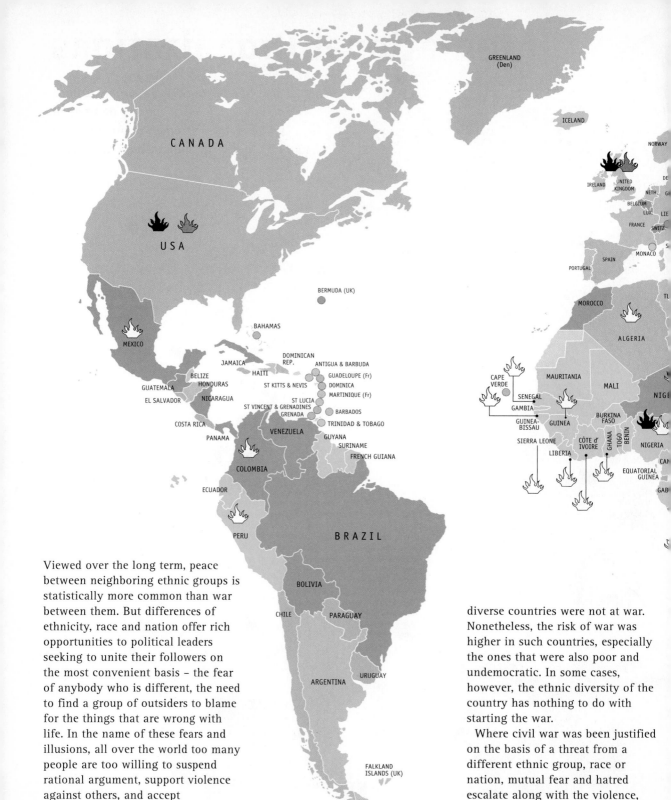

Viewed over the long term, peace between neighboring ethnic groups is statistically more common than war between them. But differences of ethnicity, race and nation offer rich opportunities to political leaders seeking to unite their followers on the most convenient basis – the fear of anybody who is different, the need to find a group of outsiders to blame for the things that are wrong with life. In the name of these fears and illusions, all over the world too many people are too willing to suspend rational argument, support violence against others, and accept restrictions on their own freedoms.

At the start of the 21st century, the majority of the most ethnically diverse countries were not at war. Nonetheless, the risk of war was higher in such countries, especially the ones that were also poor and undemocratic. In some cases, however, the ethnic diversity of the country has nothing to do with starting the war.

Where civil war was been justified on the basis of a threat from a different ethnic group, race or nation, mutual fear and hatred escalate along with the violence, making reconciliation seem a distant prospect. Then the risk of returning to warfare can be extremely high.

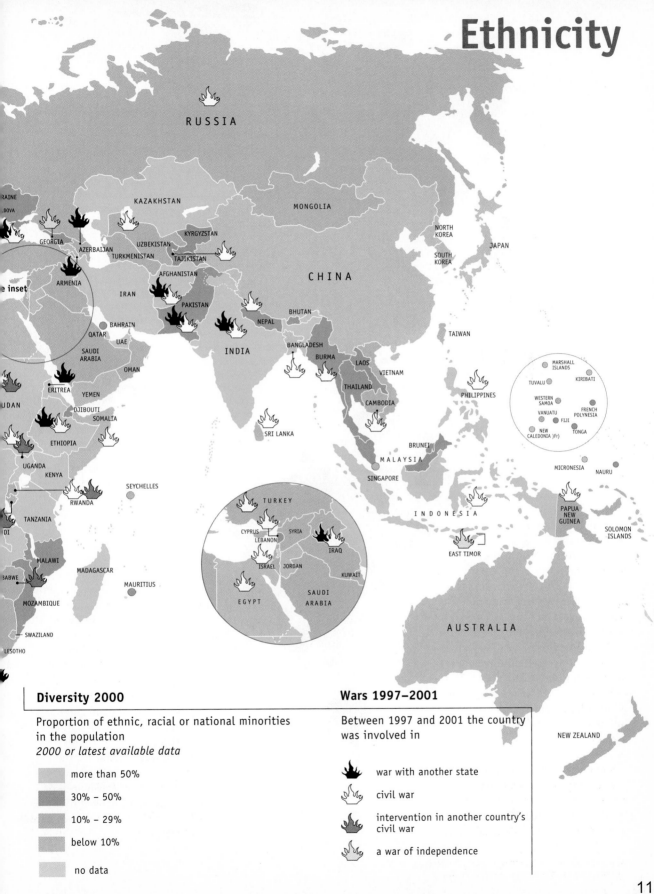

# Ethnicity

## Diversity 2000

Proportion of ethnic, racial or national minorities
in the population
*2000 or latest available data*

- more than 50%
- 30% – 50%
- 10% – 29%
- below 10%
- no data

## Wars 1997–2001

Between 1997 and 2001 the country
was involved in

- war with another state
- civil war
- intervention in another country's civil war
- a war of independence

Arbitrary arrest
and detention after
11 September 2001.

War and the extreme abuse of human rights abuse go hand in hand. At the turn of the millennium:

• There were reports of extra-judicial executions by 72 percent of states involved in civil wars.

• Of states accused of grave abuses of human rights in the form of arbitrary arrest, police and prison violence, and mistreatment of refugees and immigrants, six percent experienced civil war.

• Of states accused of torture, 30 percent experienced civil war.

• Of states accused of extra-judicial executions (of political opponents, prisoners of war and the socially undesirable), 58 percent experienced civil war.

When a state uses extreme violence, opposition to the ruling system first takes the form of silence. If the conditions that created dissatisfaction get worse, even the most extreme official violence may not suppress all opposition and then the opposition has no option but violence.

When war has started, the first instinct of most governments is to clamp down on freedoms – of information, of debate, of protest. In some cases, the clampdown becomes extreme.

From *The Penguin Atlas of War and Peace* (ISBN 0142002941)
Copyright © Myriad Editions / www.MyriadEditions.com

# Rights

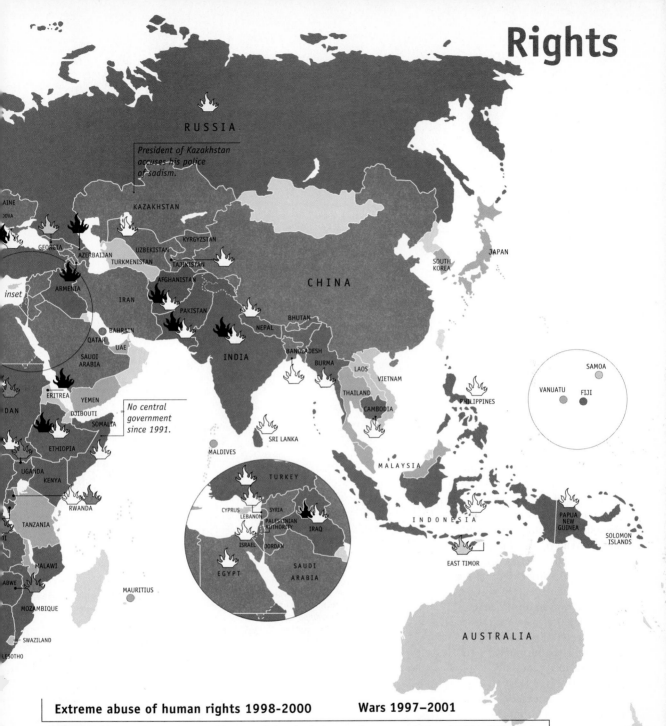

RUSSIA

*President of Kazakhstan accuses his police of sadism.*

KAZAKHSTAN

AINE

JOVA

GEORGIA

AZERBAIJAN

ARMENIA

*inset*

KYRGYZSTAN

UZBEKISTAN

TURKMENISTAN

TAJIKISTAN

AFGHANISTAN

IRAN

PAKISTAN

NEPAL

BHUTAN

BANGLADESH

CHINA

MONGOLIA

SOUTH KOREA

JAPAN

BAHRAIN

QATAR

UAE

SAUDI ARABIA

YEMEN

ERITREA

DJIBOUTI

SOMALIA

*No central government since 1991.*

DAN

ETHIOPIA

UGANDA

KENYA

RWANDA

TANZANIA

MALAWI

ABWE

MOZAMBIQUE

SWAZILAND

LESOTHO

INDIA

BURMA

LAOS

VIETNAM

THAILAND

CAMBODIA

MALDIVES

SRI LANKA

MAURITIUS

MALAYSIA

PHILIPPINES

INDONESIA

EAST TIMOR

PAPUA NEW GUINEA

SOLOMON ISLANDS

AUSTRALIA

VANUATU

SAMOA

FIJI

### Inset circle (Middle East):

TURKEY

CYPRUS

LEBANON

SYRIA

PALESTINIAN AUTHORITY

ISRAEL

JORDAN

IRAQ

EGYPT

SAUDI ARABIA

---

## Extreme abuse of human rights 1998-2000

States whose reported abuses of human rights include

- extra-judicial executions
- torture
- arbitrary arrest and detention
- mistreatment by police and/or prison authorities
- violent and/or abusive treatment of refugees, asylum seekers and/or immigrants
- no data or no human rights abuse

## Wars 1997–2001

Between 1997 and 2001 the country was involved in

 war with another state

 civil war

 intervention in another country's civil war

 a war of independence

**Employment**
Women's average wage
as percentage of men's
*2000 or latest available data*

70% and over

50% – 69%

under 50%

no data

no mandated maternity pay

In Europe, Australasia and North America, it is much less common than it used to be for women to be openly referred to as second class citizens. But polite silence on the issue cannot mask the reality that women continue, in general, to be given less well-paid jobs than men, and get paid less than men even when they are doing the same job. Likewise, although women are more present in politics than before, most political leaders are men. And outside Europe, Australasia and North America, women tend to be worse off and more excluded from power.

One of the most sensitive and controversial rights of a woman is to control her own fertility. There are about 50 million abortions a year, of which about 20 million are illegal and so unsafe that about 80,000 women each year die as a result. Emotions on the issue run deep, but the capacity of the law to regulate it satisfactorily is at least questionable. In extreme cases, opponents of abortion rights end up by committing against living people the same crime – murder – as they set out to prevent being committed against the unborn.

CANADA

USA

MEXICO

BAHAMAS

DOMINICAN REP.

JAMAICA   HAITI

BELIZE
HONDURAS
GUATEMALA
EL SALVADOR   NICARAGUA

COSTA RICA

PANAMA

TRINIDAD & TOBAGO

VENEZUELA   GUYANA

COLOMBIA

ECUADOR

PERU

BRAZIL

BOLIVIA

CHILE   PARAGUAY

ARGENTINA   URUGUAY

CAPE VERDE

*There is no country in the world where:*
• *women are a majority of the highest executive body in government*
• *women are a majority in parliament.*

**Abortion and the law**
*2002 or latest available data*

illegal or severely restricted only to save woman's life

legal to save life or preserve the health of woman and/or if the fetus is impaired

legal for social or economic reasons

legal on request but usually with gestational limits

From *The Penguin State of the World Atlas* (ISBN 0142003182)
Copyright © Myriad Editions / www.MyriadEditions.com

# Women's Rights

In many countries the relative position of women is improving, but in most countries their position is far worse than men's.

## Popular religions
Majority religion or denomination

### Buddhism

Mahayana    Theravada

Chinese    Tibetan    Japanese

### Christianity

Protestantism

Lutheranism   Anglicanism   Calvinism   Roman Catholicism   Orthodox

Congregationalism   Methodism   Baptist   Presbyterianism

Dutch Reform Church

### Islam

Sunni    Shia    Ibadiyyah

Hanafi   Hanbali   Maliki   Shafi

Ithna'ashaariyya    Zaydis

### Other religions

Hinduism

Judaism

atheism

Chinese indigenous religion

other indigenous beliefs

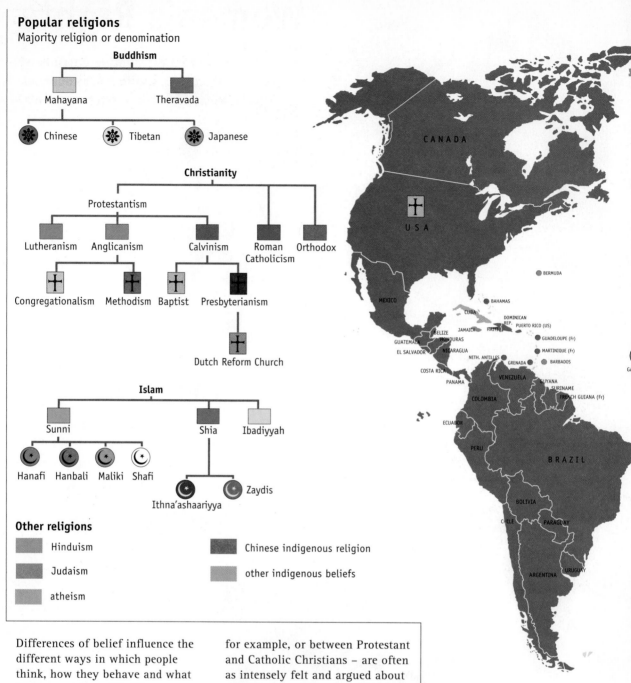

CANADA

USA

BERMUDA

MEXICO

BAHAMAS

CUBA

DOMINICAN REP.

PUERTO RICO (US)

BELIZE

JAMAICA

HAITI

GUATEMALA

HONDURAS

GUADELOUPE (Fr)

EL SALVADOR

NICARAGUA

MARTINIQUE (Fr)

NETH. ANTILLES

GRENADA

BARBADOS

COSTA RICA

VENEZUELA

GUYANA

PANAMA

SURINAME

FRENCH GUIANA (Fr)

COLOMBIA

ECUADOR

PERU

BRAZIL

BOLIVIA

CHILE

PARAGUAY

ARGENTINA

URUGUAY

GAM

---

Differences of belief influence the different ways in which people think, how they behave and what they expect from life. They are among the deepest cultural differences.

The impressive statistics for the number said to belong to one religion or another mask the many schisms within the major religions. Differences within religions – between Sunni and Shia Muslims,

for example, or between Protestant and Catholic Christians – are often as intensely felt and argued about as differences between them.

The numbers also hide the difference between practising believers and those who merely claim adherence to a faith but do little to express it. In western Europe, for example, far more people profess a faith than practice it.

From *The Penguin State of the World Atlas* (ISBN 0142003182)
Copyright © Myriad Editions / www.MyriadEditions.com

# Beliefs

The world's largest religions are Christianity (about 2 billion believers) and Islam (just over 1 billion).

80% of the world's population profess a religious belief, but far fewer practice their religion

## Population size
Countries' share of world population

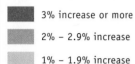

☐ = 1%
☐ = 0.1%
☐ = 0.01%

## Population change
Rate of annual change
*2002*

- ■ 3% increase or more
- ■ 2% – 2.9% increase
- ■ 1% – 1.9% increase
- ☐ under 1% increase
- ■ decrease

The world's population doubled in the second half of the 20th century, passing 6 billion at the start of the 21st. The rate of growth has slowed, especially in the two most populous countries – China and India – but on current trends the total will top 9 billion in 2050, with Africa and parts of the Middle East growing fastest.

As population growth slows and even declines in the richer countries, the average age rises. Then, the economically active must support not only themselves but a rising number of older people. The result is a looming welfare crisis.

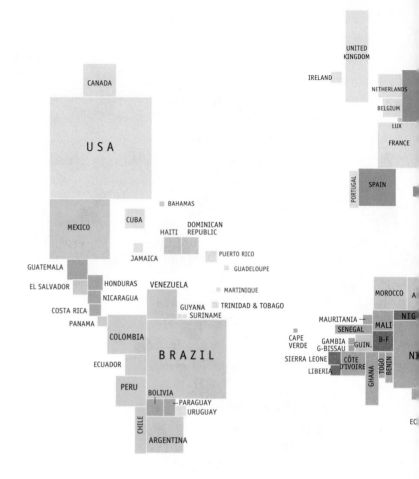

## Future populations
Percentage of population by age-range
*2000 and 2050*

- ● 60 years and over
- ● 40 – 59 years
- ● 20 – 29 years
- ● up to 19 years

| | Brazil | USA | UK |
|---|---|---|---|
| **2000** | 8% / 18% / 35% / 39% | 16% / 26% / 29% / 29% | 20% / 26% / 29% / 25% |
| **2050** | 28% / 27% / 24% / 21% | 26% / 23% / 25% / 26% | 32% / 25% / 23% / 20% |

From *The Penguin State of the World Atlas* (ISBN 0142003182)
Copyright © Myriad Editions / www.MyriadEditions.com

# Population

**As countries get richer, the population grows more slowly.**

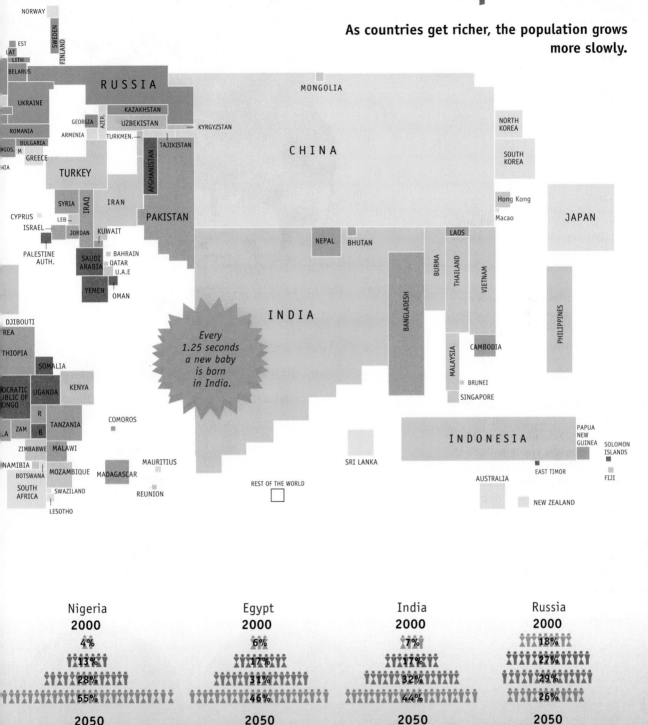

NORWAY
EST
LAT
LITH
SWEDEN
FINLAND
BELARUS
RUSSIA
MONGOLIA
UKRAINE
KAZAKHSTAN
KYRGYZSTAN
NORTH KOREA
GEORGIA
AZER.
UZBEKISTAN
ARMENIA
TURKMEN.
TAJIKISTAN
CHINA
SOUTH KOREA
ROMANIA
GOS.
M
BULGARIA
GREECE
NIA
TURKEY
AFGHANISTAN
CYPRUS
SYRIA
IRAQ
IRAN
LEB.
JORDAN
KUWAIT
PAKISTAN
Hong Kong
Macao
JAPAN
ISRAEL
PALESTINE AUTH.
SAUDI ARABIA
BAHRAIN
QATAR
U.A.E
YEMEN
OMAN
NEPAL
BHUTAN
LAOS
BURMA
THAILAND
VIETNAM
DJIBOUTI
REA
THIOPIA
SOMALIA
INDIA
BANGLADESH
MALAYSIA
CAMBODIA
PHILIPPINES
OCRATIC UBLIC OF ONGO
UGANDA
KENYA
R
ZAM
B
TANZANIA
COMOROS
BRUNEI
SINGAPORE
ZIMBABWE
MALAWI
A
INDONESIA
PAPUA NEW GUINEA
SOLOMON ISLANDS
NAMIBIA
BOTSWANA
MOZAMBIQUE
MADAGASCAR
MAURITIUS
SRI LANKA
EAST TIMOR
FIJI
SOUTH AFRICA
SWAZILAND
REUNION
REST OF THE WORLD
AUSTRALIA
NEW ZEALAND
LESOTHO

*Every 1.25 seconds a new baby is born in India.*

| Nigeria | Egypt | India | Russia |
|---|---|---|---|
| **2000** | **2000** | **2000** | **2000** |
| 4% | 6% | 7% | 18% |
| 13% | 17% | 17% | 27% |
| 28% | 31% | 32% | 29% |
| 55% | 46% | 44% | 26% |
| **2050** | **2050** | **2050** | **2050** |
| 8% | 20% | 20% | 35% |
| 20% | 26% | 26% | 24% |
| 33% | 27% | 27% | 23% |
| 39% | 27% | 27% | 18% |

19

## Energy consumption

Average energy used per person
*2000*
unit equal to energy produced
by a tonne of oil

- over 10.0
- 5.1 – 10.0
- 2.6 – 5.0
- 1.1 – 2.5
- 0.1 – 1.0
- no data

Energy can be bought, sold and fought over. It is a highly varied and wholly essential commodity, without which nothing can be done.

As countries get richer they consume more energy per person, until their economies shift from manufacturing to the information and service sectors. Then, energy efficiency increases and consumption tends to decline.

Almost all energy consumed comes from coal, gas, oil or uranium. These non-renewable energy sources create pollution, risk major accidents, and cannot be sustained in the long term.

Renewable energy sources – using the power of the wind, waves and sun as well as hydro-electricity – are being used in some countries. They could be used worldwide when companies find them more profitable, or when governments opt for safer energy.

## Over 90% of energy used comes from non-renewable sources

## World energy production

Percentage of energy produced
by each type of fuel
*2000*

**1973**

nuclear 1%
renewable sources 4%
gas 19%
coal 23%
oil 53%

**2000**

nuclear 6%
renewable sources 11%
oil 41%
gas 22%
coal 20%

From *The Penguin State of the World Atlas* (ISBN 0142003182)
Copyright © Myriad Editions / www.MyriadEditions.com

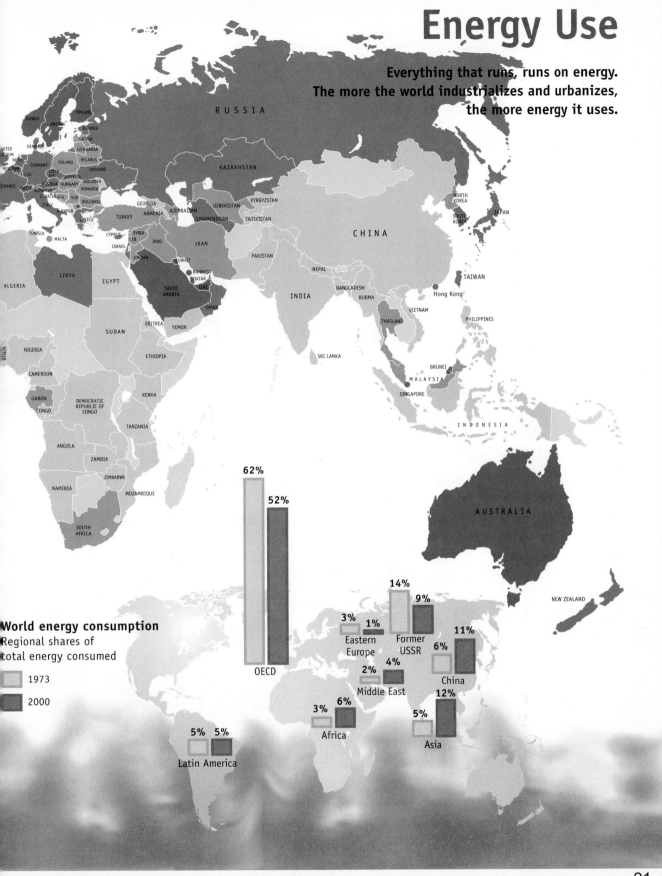

# Energy Use

Everything that runs, runs on energy.
The more the world industrializes and urbanizes,
the more energy it uses.

**World energy consumption**
Regional shares of
total energy consumed

1973

2000

62% 52%
OECD

14% 9%
Former
USSR

3% 1%
Eastern
Europe

2% 4%
Middle East

6% 11%
China

3% 6%
Africa

5% 12%
Asia

5% 5%
Latin America

At the end of the 20th century approximately 40 million people had fled their homes for fear of war and persecution. Of these, just over 14 million have fled abroad, thus fulfilling the international definition of "refugee". At least six million live in a state of limbo, neither legally recognised as refugees, nor able to return home. About 20 million have found refuge inside their own countries: they may not have suffered less than the others, but they are likely to return home more quickly.

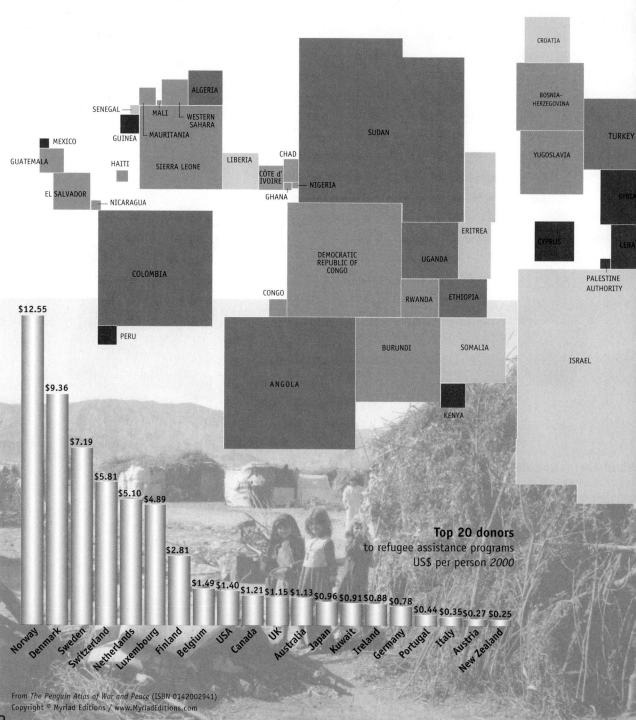

CROATIA

BOSNIA-HERZEGOVINA

ALGERIA

SENEGAL

MALI

WESTERN SAHARA

GUINEA

MAURITANIA

TURKEY

YUGOSLAVIA

MEXICO

HAITI

SUDAN

GUATEMALA

SIERRA LEONE

LIBERIA

CHAD

CÔTE d' IVOIRE

NIGERIA

GHANA

EL SALVADOR

NICARAGUA

ERITREA

SYRIA

CYPRUS

LEBA

DEMOCRATIC REPUBLIC OF CONGO

UGANDA

COLOMBIA

CONGO

RWANDA

ETHIOPIA

PALESTINE AUTHORITY

PERU

BURUNDI

SOMALIA

ISRAEL

ANGOLA

KENYA

**Top 20 donors**
to refugee assistance programs
US$ per person *2000*

$12.55 Norway
$9.36 Denmark
$7.19 Sweden
$5.81 Switzerland
$5.10 Netherlands
$4.89 Luxembourg
$2.81 Finland
$1.49 Belgium
$1.40 USA
$1.21 Canada
$1.15 UK
$1.13 Australia
$0.96 Japan
$0.91 Kuwait
$0.88 Ireland
$0.78 Germany
$0.44 Portugal
$0.35 Italy
$0.27 Austria
$0.25 New Zealand

From *The Penguin Atlas of War and Peace* (ISBN 0142002941)
Copyright © Myriad Editions / www.MyriadEditions.com

# Refugees

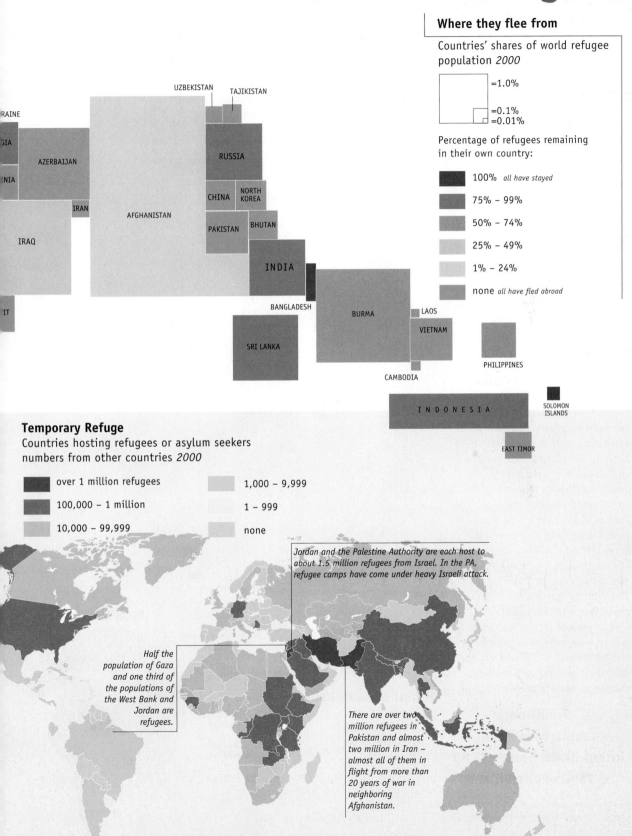

## Where they flee from

Countries' shares of world refugee population *2000*

- ⬜ =1.0%
- =0.1%
- =0.01%

Percentage of refugees remaining in their own country:

- 100% *all have stayed*
- 75% – 99%
- 50% – 74%
- 25% – 49%
- 1% – 24%
- none *all have fled abroad*

UZBEKISTAN
TAJIKISTAN
RAINE
GIA
AZERBAIJAN
ENIA
IRAN
RUSSIA
AFGHANISTAN
CHINA
NORTH KOREA
IRAQ
PAKISTAN
BHUTAN
IT
INDIA
BANGLADESH
BURMA
LAOS
VIETNAM
SRI LANKA
CAMBODIA
PHILIPPINES
INDONESIA
SOLOMON ISLANDS
EAST TIMOR

## Temporary Refuge

Countries hosting refugees or asylum seekers numbers from other countries *2000*

- over 1 million refugees
- 100,000 – 1 million
- 10,000 – 99,999
- 1,000 – 9,999
- 1 – 999
- none

*Jordan and the Palestine Authority are each host to about 1.5 million refugees from Israel. In the PA, refugee camps have come under heavy Israeli attack.*

*Half the population of Gaza and one third of the populations of the West Bank and Jordan are refugees.*

*There are over two million refugees in Pakistan and almost two million in Iran – almost all of them in flight from more than 20 years of war in neighboring Afghanistan.*

## Wars since the Cold War
*1990–March 2003*

states involved in armed conflict *since 1990*

other states

### Location of wars

war *2002–2003*

recent war *since 1990*

recent tension *since 1990*

The end of the Cold War was the end of an era of international relations. As the USSR and former Yugoslavia broke up, the number of wars each year increased sharply. The international news media started to report the extraordinary cruelty displayed in many of the wars, especially in Bosnia-Herzegovina and Chechnya, and worst of all in Rwanda, where 800,000 people were massacred in a six-week period in 1994.

Under 10 percent of today's wars are between states. The pattern of most civil wars is one of bursts of activity alternating with long periods of relative calm. As a result, most wars stay out of the news media most of the time. Over half of today's civil wars have lasted more than five years; in long-lasting conflicts, it is not just the original causes that keep the war going, but the harm each side has done to the other and the pain and bitterness that result.

The symbols on the map show where wars were being fought in the 1990s and in 2002–3 but do not show how many wars were fought in each country or region.

**7 million people have been killed in wars since 1989 – 75% were civilians**

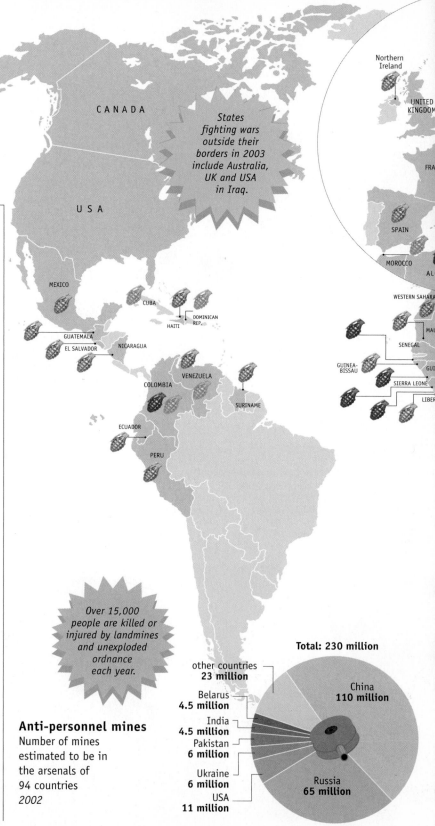

States fighting wars outside their borders in 2003 include Australia, UK and USA in Iraq.

Over 15,000 people are killed or injured by landmines and unexploded ordnance each year.

**Anti-personnel mines**
Number of mines estimated to be in the arsenals of 94 countries *2002*

**Total: 230 million**

other countries **23 million**
Belarus **4.5 million**
India **4.5 million**
Pakistan **6 million**
Ukraine **6 million**
USA **11 million**

China **110 million**

Russia **65 million**

From *The Penguin State of the World Atlas* (ISBN 0142003182)
Copyright © Myriad Editions / www.MyriadEditions.com

# War

There have been 125 wars worldwide since the end of the Cold War in late 1989.

RUSSIA
Moscow

Ingushetia/
North Ossetia

Chechnya

Dagestan

RUSSIA

SLOVENIA
MOLDOVA
B-H
YUGOSLAVIA
ALBANIA
MACEDONIA
GREECE

Nagorno-
Karabakh

UZBEKISTAN

see inset

GEORGIA
ARMENIA
AZERBAIJAN

TAJIKISTAN

NORTH
KOREA

AFGHANISTAN

Punjab

CHINA

IRAN

Assam,
Manipur,
Tripura

PAKISTAN

Nagaland

TAIWAN

NEPAL

BANGLADESH

INDIA
BURMA

LAOS

ER
CHAD
SUDAN
ERITREA
YEMEN

DJIBOUTI

Andra Pradesh

Spratly
Islands

PHILIPPINES

CAMBODIA

A
CENTRAL
AFRICAN REP.
ETHIOPIA
SOMALIA

SRI LANKA

Phnom Penh

CONGO
UGANDA
RWANDA
BURUNDI

Aceh

Bougainville
Island

DEMOCRATIC
REPUBLIC OF
CONGO

Moluccas

INDONESIA

West Papua

PAPUA
NEW
GUINEA

ANGOLA

MALAWI

MADAGASCAR

EAST TIMOR

ZIMBABWE

NAMIBIA

MOZAMBIQUE

AUSTRALIA

SOUTH
AFRICA
LESOTHO

TURKEY

CYPRUS
LEBANON
ISRAEL
Cairo
EGYPT

SYRIA
IRAQ
KUWAIT
SAUDI
ARABIA

## War since the Cold War
Number of wars
each year *1990–2002*

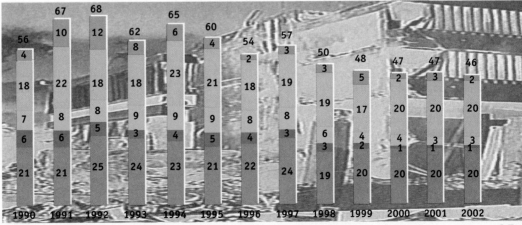

- Europe
- Sub-Saharan Africa
- North Africa & Middle East
- Central & South America
- Asia & Pacific

| | 1990 | 1991 | 1992 | 1993 | 1994 | 1995 | 1996 | 1997 | 1998 | 1999 | 2000 | 2001 | 2002 |
|---|---|---|---|---|---|---|---|---|---|---|---|---|---|
| Total | 56 | 67 | 68 | 62 | 65 | 60 | 54 | 57 | 50 | 48 | 47 | 47 | 46 |
| Europe | 4 | 10 | 12 | 8 | 6 | 4 | 2 | 3 | 3 | 5 | 2 | 3 | 2 |
| Sub-Saharan Africa | 18 | 22 | 18 | 18 | 23 | 21 | 18 | 19 | 19 | 17 | 20 | 20 | 20 |
| North Africa & Middle East | 7 | 8 | 8 | 9 | 9 | 9 | 8 | 8 | 6 | 4 | 4 | 3 | 3 |
| Central & South America | 6 | 6 | 5 | 3 | 5 | 4 | 4 | 3 | 3 | 2 | 1 | 1 | 1 |
| Asia & Pacific | 21 | 21 | 25 | 24 | 23 | 21 | 22 | 24 | 19 | 20 | 20 | 20 | 20 |

## Terrorist actions

IRELAND
UNITED KINGDOM
FRANCE
AL
ITAL
SPAIN
ALGERIA
GUINEA
SIERRA LEONE
LIBERIA

USA

PANAMA
COLOMBIA
PERU

ARGENTINA

New York and Washington DC 2001
August 6 *According to press reports, President Bush was given an intelligence briefing predicting terrorist group al Qaida planned to hijack aircraft, probably to use in attacks on the USA.*
September 11 *World Trade Center and Pentagon hit by hijacked aircraft: 3,200 killed.*

Terrorism is usually the tactic of the force that is weaker than its enemy. The weapons of terrorism are assassinations of political leaders and indiscriminate attacks on civilians, usually with bombs.

Discussion of terrorism is full of moral outrage and fear because it is cloaked in secrecy and attacks either ordinary citizens or political leaders. Yet it is hard to see what is more outrageous or frightening about a bomb placed under a car or in a bus, than a missile that comes out of the sky. War is hell when it strikes, regardless of how it strikes.

In historical perspective, it is not only rebels who have used terrorism. The term was invented to describe a government strategy of rule by terror, and state terrorism has been as common as anti-state terrorism for the last two centuries. Even today, when use of the term is almost exclusively reserved for insurrectionaries, the terrorist tactic of assassination is used as much by governments as against them.

# Terrorism

**Moscow 2002**
*Chechen guerrillas held several hundred theatre-goers hostage: over 100 were accidentally gassed to death by Russian forces in the rescue mission; 50 guerrillas killed.*

RUSSIA

GEORGIA

UZBEKISTAN  KYRGYZSTAN

TAJIKISTAN

IRAN  AFGHANISTAN

PAKISTAN

set

JDAN

YEMEN

SOMALIA

ETHIOPIA

UGANDA

KENYA

TANZANIA

INDIA

BANGLADESH

**Yemen 2002**
*US remote-controlled missile: 6 al Qaida suspects killed.*

SRI LANKA

JAPAN

**Tokyo 1995**
*Nerve gas attack in subway by Aum Shinrikyo cult: 11 killed.*

PHILIPPINES

CAMBODIA

MALAYSIA

SINGAPORE

INDONESIA

**Nairobi and Dar es Salaam 1998**
*Al Qaida attacks on US embassies: 224 people killed, including 12 Americans, and over 4,000 injured.*

TURKEY

SYRIA

LEBANON

ISRAEL

IRAQ

PALESTINE AUTHORITY

JORDAN

EGYPT

KUWAIT

**Bali 2002**
*Nightclub bombing: 200 holidaymakers and locals killed.*

There are far fewer nuclear weapons now than there were at the height of the Cold War. Their destructive power remains unimaginable – one modestly sized nuclear weapon can destroy a major city. Many experts believe that the greatest risk of nuclear war is in the confrontation between the two smallest and newest nuclear powers – India and Pakistan.

## Nuclear stockpiles
The world total of nuclear warheads in 2001 was approximately 19,000, down from about 50,000 in 1985 at the height of the Cold War.

Russia
**9,196**

## Satellites
by 2010:

**4 High Level Space-Based Infra-Red System satellites** for detecting the launching of missiles against the USA

**24 Low Level Space-Based Infra-Red System satellites** for tracking the flight paths of missiles launched against the USA

## Radars
by 2007:
**1 new** on Shemya Island (Aleutians) off Alaska
**5 upgraded:** Alaska, California, Massachusetts Fylingdales, UK (needs UK government permission) Thule, Greenland (needs Danish government permission)

by 2010:
**9 new**, location unknown yet, may include Japan & South Korea

**Ground-based interceptors (missiles)** Alaska **100** by 2007; North Dakota additional **150** in 2010

**Command and Control** Cheyenne Mountain, Colorado

US Department of Defense Major Range and Test Facility Base, Kwajalein Atoll, Marshall Islands

## National Missile Defense
The USA was so keen on its plan to deploy a missile defense system that it was willing to break the 1972 Anti-Ballistic Missile Treaty. When Russia agreed in 2002 to abandon its opposition this agreement, long regarded as the cornerstone of strategic stability, the doubts and disagreements among the USA's major allies became much less important and the US government moved quickly to start deployment. The cost of the full system is an estimated $60 billion by 2015.

From *The Penguin Atlas of War and Peace* (ISBN 0142002941)
Copyright © Myriad Editions / www.MyriadEditions.com

# Mass Destruction

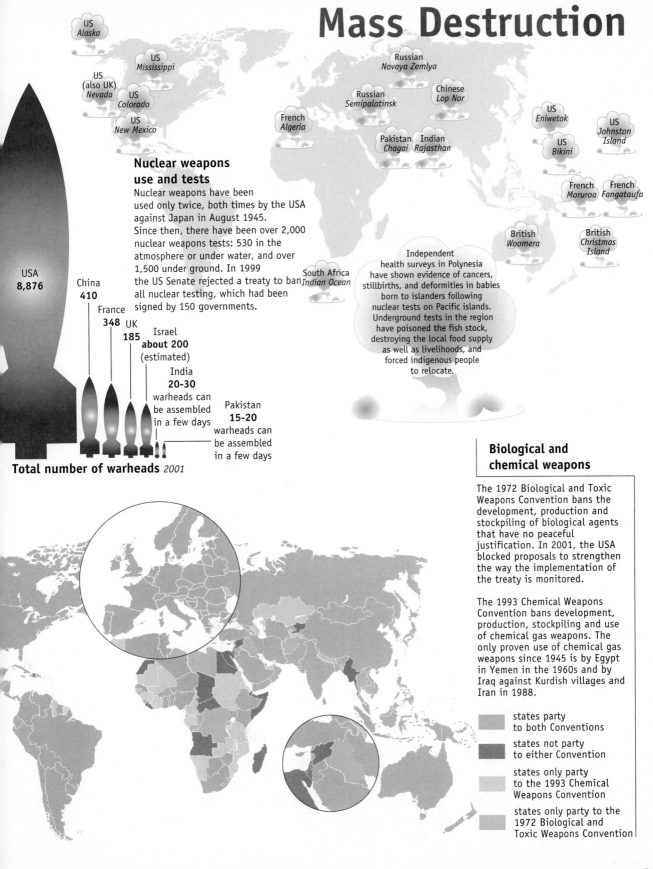

**US** *Alaska*

**US** *Mississippi*

**US** *(also UK)* *Nevada*

**US** *Colorado*

**US** *New Mexico*

**French** *Algeria*

**Russian** *Novaya Zemlya*

**Russian** *Semipalatinsk*

**Chinese** *Lop Nor*

**US** *Eniwetok*

**US** *Bikini*

**US** *Johnston Island*

**Pakistan** *Chagai*  **Indian** *Rajasthan*

**French** *Moruroa*  **French** *Fangataufa*

**British** *Woomera*

**British** *Christmas Island*

**South Africa** *Indian Ocean*

## Nuclear weapons use and tests

Nuclear weapons have been used only twice, both times by the USA against Japan in August 1945. Since then, there have been over 2,000 nuclear weapons tests: 530 in the atmosphere or under water, and over 1,500 under ground. In 1999 the US Senate rejected a treaty to ban all nuclear testing, which had been signed by 150 governments.

Independent health surveys in Polynesia have shown evidence of cancers, stillbirths, and deformities in babies born to islanders following nuclear tests on Pacific islands. Underground tests in the region have poisoned the fish stock, destroying the local food supply as well as livelihoods, and forced indigenous people to relocate.

**USA** **8,876**

**China** **410**

**France** **348**

**UK** **185**

**Israel** **about 200** (estimated)

**India** **20-30** warheads can be assembled in a few days

**Pakistan** **15-20** warheads can be assembled in a few days

### Total number of warheads *2001*

## Biological and chemical weapons

The 1972 Biological and Toxic Weapons Convention bans the development, production and stockpiling of biological agents that have no peaceful justification. In 2001, the USA blocked proposals to strengthen the way the implementation of the treaty is monitored.

The 1993 Chemical Weapons Convention bans development, production, stockpiling and use of chemical gas weapons. The only proven use of chemical gas weapons since 1945 is by Egypt in Yemen in the 1960s and by Iraq against Kurdish villages and Iran in 1988.

states party to both Conventions

states not party to either Convention

states only party to the 1993 Chemical Weapons Convention

states only party to the 1972 Biological and Toxic Weapons Convention

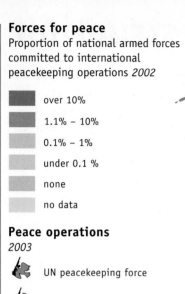

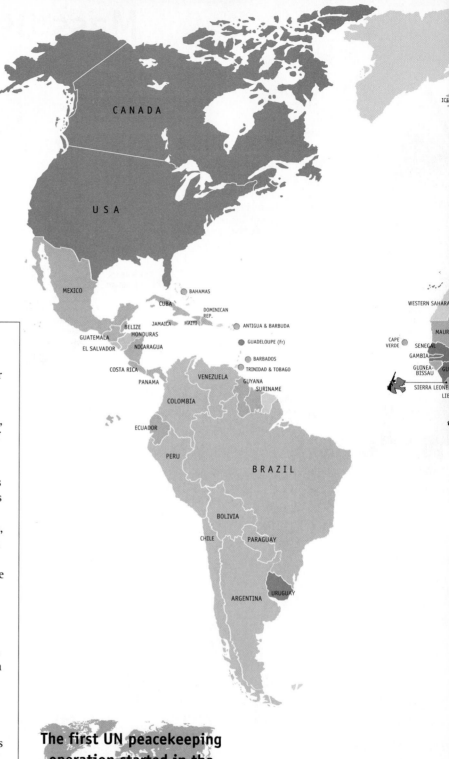

Before 1990, the UN mounted 15 peace operations. It mounted the same number in the next four years. Today, UN and other peacekeeping operations involve about 250,000 military personnel, which is a little over 1 percent of regular armed forces worldwide.

Peacekeeping operations began as a way of monitoring ceasefires and peace agreements. The troops in such operations are observers and monitors rather than fighters, and have no weapons larger than small arms, which they can only use in self-defence, when they are already being fired on and their lives are in danger.

Over the years, more complex tasks have been added, including the protection of civilians in war, which went disastrously wrong in Bosnia-Herzegovina in 1995, when peacekeepers could do nothing to prevent the massacre of 7,000 Bosniaks in Srebrenica. Helping rebuild war-torn societies is now often part of the duties of peacekeeping forces.

**The first UN peacekeeping operation started in the Middle East in 1948. It is still going**

From *The Penguin State of the World Atlas* (ISBN 0142003182)
Copyright © Myriad Editions / www.MyriadEditions.com

# Peacekeeping

UN peacekeeping operations monitor ceasefires, implement peace agreements and protect civilians. They have been mounted with increasing frequency since the end of the Cold War.

**Fifty years of trying to keep the peace**
Number of UN peacekeeping operations
*1950–2000* selected years

2
1950

4
1960

4
1970

6
1980

10
1990

18
2000

## Purchasing power

GDP per person
*2000*
PPP US$

*A PPP (Purchasing Power Parity) dollar has the same purchasing power in the domestic economy as $1 has in the USA.*

- $20,000 and over
- $10,000 – $19,999
- $5,000 – $9,999
- $1,000 – $4,999
- under $1,000
- no data

**Highest:** Luxembourg $50,061, USA $34,142
**Lowest:** Sierra Leone $490, Tanzania $523

Average annual change in GDP per person
*1990–2000*

- increase of 4% or more
- decrease of 4% or more

Gross Domestic (or National) Product (GDP/GNP) is the most common way of measuring a country's wealth. It combines the value of goods (the things people make, grow or extract from the ground and then sell) and services (things people do for money). It measures the wealth in a country, but not how the wealth is distributed or used (see pages 42 and 48). Nonetheless, this crude measure of national wealth does give a broad indication of the stage of economic development reached by a country, and enables comparisons to be made between countries and across continents. It thus gives an idea of the different economic circumstances within which a government and people are working.

**The average inhabitant of the world's richest country is over 100 times wealthier than the average inhabitant of the poorest**

From *The Penguin State of the World Atlas* (ISBN 0142003182)
Copyright © Myriad Editions / www.MyriadEditions.com

# National Income

**The global wealth gap keeps on growing.**

FINLAND
ESTONIA
LATVIA
LITHUANIA
RUSSIA
BELARUS
POLAND
SLOVAKIA
UKRAINE
HUNGARY
ROMANIA
MOLDOVA
BULGARIA
ALBANIA MACEDONIA
GREECE

**5**
**-9**
**-10**
**4**

RUSSIA **-5**

KAZAKHSTAN

**-12** GEORGIA
**-7** ARMENIA
AZERBAIJAN **-8** TURKMENISTAN
UZBEKISTAN
**-5** KYRGYZSTAN
TAJIKISTAN **-12**

MONGOLIA

**9** CHINA

JAPAN

SOUTH KOREA **5**

TURKEY
CYPRUS
SYRIA
LEBANON ISRAEL
PALESTINE AUTHORITY
JORDAN
IRAN
KUWAIT
BAHRAIN
SAUDI ARABIA
UAE

EGYPT

PAKISTAN

NEPAL BHUTAN
BANGLADESH

**4** INDIA

Hong Kong

SUDAN **6**
ERITREA
YEMEN
ETHIOPIA

BURMA **5**
LAOS
THAILAND
VIETNAM
CAMBODIA **6**

PHILIPPINES

VANUATU SAMOA
FIJI

CHAD

NIGER
NIGERIA
CAMEROON
GABON
CONGO
CENTRAL AFRICAN REP.
DEMOCRATIC REPUBLIC OF CONGO **-8**
UGANDA
RWANDA
BURUNDI
KENYA
TANZANIA **-5**

SRI LANKA

MALDIVES **5**

COMOROS

ANGOLA
ZAMBIA
MALAWI
ZIMBABWE
MOZAMBIQUE
NAMIBIA
BOTSWANA
SWAZILAND
SOUTH AFRICA
LESOTHO

MADAGASCAR **4** MAURITIUS

MALAYSIA **4** BRUNEI
SINGAPORE **5**

INDONESIA

PAPUA NEW GUINEA
SOLOMON ISLANDS

AUSTRALIA

NEW ZEALAND

BAHAMAS
SAINT KITTS & NEVIS
ST VINCENT & GRENADINES DOMINICA
GRENADA SAINT LUCIA BARBADOS
TRINIDAD & TOBAGO
CAPE VERDE
MALTA
BAHRAIN
Hong Kong
VANUATU SAMOA
FIJI
MALDIVES
SINGAPORE
SEYCHELLES
MAURITIUS

## Inflation
Average annual change in consumer price index
*1990–2000*

- 100% and over
- 10 – 99%
- under 10%
- no data

33

## Service sector

Percentage of GDP generated by services
*1998 or latest available data*

- 60% and over
- 50–59%
- 40–49%
- 30–39%
- 20–29%
- no data

**+176%** increase of 30% and over
*1998 compared with 1980*

**-37%** decrease of 20% and over
*1998 compared with 1980*

CANADA

UNITED STATES OF AMERICA

MEXICO

JAMAICA

GUATEMALA
HONDURAS
NICARAGUA

DOMINICAN REPUBLIC
HAITI

**+50%**
EL SALVADOR
COSTA RICA
PANAMA

VENEZUELA
TRINIDAD & TOBAGO

COLOMBIA

ECUADOR

PERU

BRAZIL
**+40%**

BOLIVIA

PARAGUAY

CHILE

URUGUAY
ARGENTINA

IRELAND
UNITED KINGDOM

SPAIN

MOROCCO

**-30%**
GUINEA-BISSAU

SIERRA

The last three decades of the 20th century saw dramatic changes in the way we live – an Information Revolution, some people call it.

In terms of technology, the Information Revolution refers to the possibilities opened up by digitization: the power of computers to store, manipulate and transmit information in the form of speech, data and video more compactly, more cheaply and at greater speed than ever before. This capacity enabled three previously separate industries – telecommunications, electronics (including the electronic media) and computing – to converge as a new juggernaut known as Information Technology, or IT. The variety, sophistication and sheer number of IT devices introduced into our working lives and our homes led to excited talk about entering a new Information Age, supposedly as radically different from the Industrial Age as that was from the agricultural societies that preceded it.

What has changed – economically, socially and culturally? Do the changes really represent an epochal shift? Has the technology caused the changes, or has its availability simply accelerated trends that were already underway? Will IT be as important historically as steam power or electricity were in the Industrial Revolution?

In economic terms, the most striking thing about IT has been the unprecedented coincidence of increasing power with falling costs. It took from the 1790s until 1850 for the price of steam power to halve. The price of electricity fell by 65 percent between 1890 and 1930, a decline of no more than 2 to 3 percent a year. In comparison, the price of computer processing power has fallen by an average of 30 percent a year over the past 20 years, and is now just 0.01 percent of its level in the early 1970s. This astonishing reduction in cost has accelerated the global spread of the "information highway".

New information and communication technologies have changed the way we work, allowing greater control over the processes of production and distribution. To what extent they have caused changes in the type of work we do is more debatable. In the advanced industrial nations the growth of IT has coincided with the growth of the service sector – an elastic category that can include anything from stock-broking, librarianship, computer maintenance or journalism to belly-dancing. Whether IT has caused this shift, which was already apparent in the USA in the 1950s (see right), is open to question. In countries such as China and Thailand, where nearly half the working population is still employed on the land, the transition is bound to be slower.

From *The Penguin Atlas of Media and Information* (ISBN 0142000175)
Copyright © Myriad Editions / www.MyriadEditions.com

# The Information Society

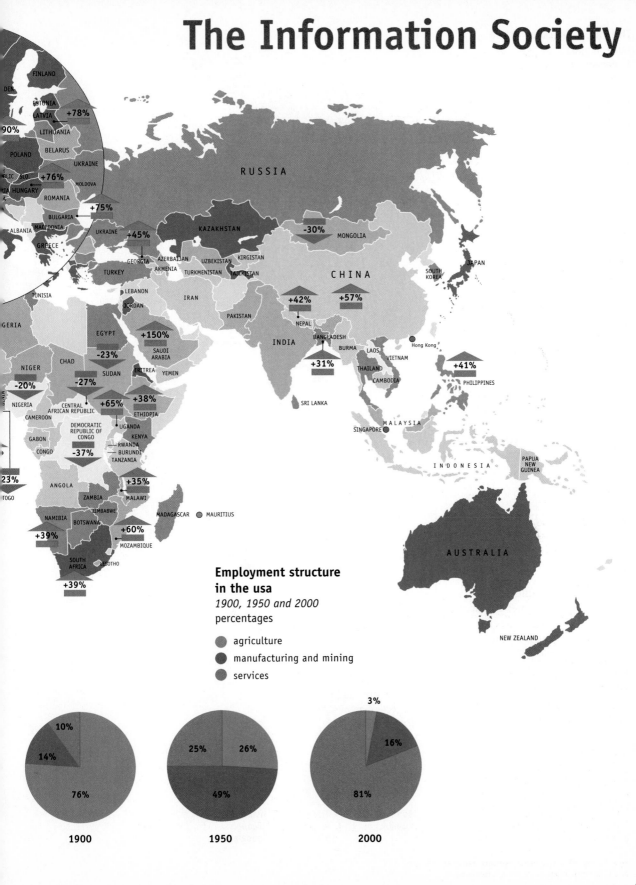

FINLAND

DEN

ESTONIA

LATVIA +78%

90%

LITHUANIA

POLAND   BELARUS

UKRAINE

BLIC  SLO +76%

HUNGARY   MOLDOVA

ROMANIA

BULGARIA +75%

ALBANIA MACEDONIA

GREECE

UKRAINE +45%

GEORGIA AZERBAIJAN UZBEKISTAN KIRGISTAN

ARMENIA TURKMENISTAN TAJIKISTAN

TURKEY

TUNISIA

RUSSIA

KAZAKHSTAN

-30%   MONGOLIA

CHINA

JAPAN

SOUTH KOREA

GERIA

LEBANON

JORDAN

IRAN

PAKISTAN

+42%   +57%

NEPAL

EGYPT +150%

-23%

SAUDI ARABIA

INDIA

BANGLADESH

BURMA   LAOS   Hong Kong

+31%   THAILAND   VIETNAM

+41%

NIGER   CHAD   SUDAN   ERITREA   YEMEN   CAMBODIA

-20%   -27%

NIGERIA   CENTRAL AFRICAN REPUBLIC   +65%   +38%

CAMEROON   ETHIOPIA

PHILIPPINES

SRI LANKA

DEMOCRATIC REPUBLIC OF CONGO   UGANDA   KENYA

GABON   RWANDA

CONGO   -37%   BURUNDI   TANZANIA

MALAYSIA

SINGAPORE

23%

TOGO

ANGOLA   +35%

ZAMBIA   MALAWI

ZIMBABWE

NAMIBIA   MADAGASCAR   MAURITIUS

BOTSWANA   +60%

+39%   MOZAMBIQUE

SOUTH AFRICA   LESOTHO

+39%

INDONESIA

PAPUA NEW GUINEA

AUSTRALIA

NEW ZEALAND

## Employment structure in the usa
*1900, 1950 and 2000*
percentages

● agriculture
● manufacturing and mining
● services

| 1900 | 1950 | 2000 |
|------|------|------|
| 10% 14% 76% | 25% 26% 49% | 3% 16% 81% |

## The importance of trade

Trade in goods
as percentage of GDP
*2000*

- over 100%
- 76% – 100%
- 51% – 75%
- 26% – 50%
- 1% – 25%
- no data

## Change in trade as share of GDP

*1980–1999*

- increase of 100% or more
- decrease of 10% or more

Some countries are so dependent on exports and imports that the value of their international trade exceeds that of their Gross Domestic Product. And with globalization, many of the wealthier counties have experienced a major increase in the scale of their international trade, which has grown much faster than their economies overall. Yet the USA, the powerhouse of the world economy and the fulcrum on which many economies balance (or come unbalanced) has a relatively low engagement in international trade. This gives the USA stability and a capacity to recover quickly from the downturn at the end of one economic cycle, ready for the start of the next cycle.

Countries with small economies, heavy trade dependence and reliance on agriculture have been hit by a change in the world market that has made fertilizers more expensive relative to agricultural products.

## Bloc trade

Trade within trading blocs
as percentage of total export
of each trade bloc
*2001*

- 61% European Union
- 60% Free Trade Area of the Americas
- 73% Asia Pacific Economic Cooperation

From *The Penguin State of the World Atlas* (ISBN 0142003182)
Copyright © Myriad Editions / www.MyriadEditions.com

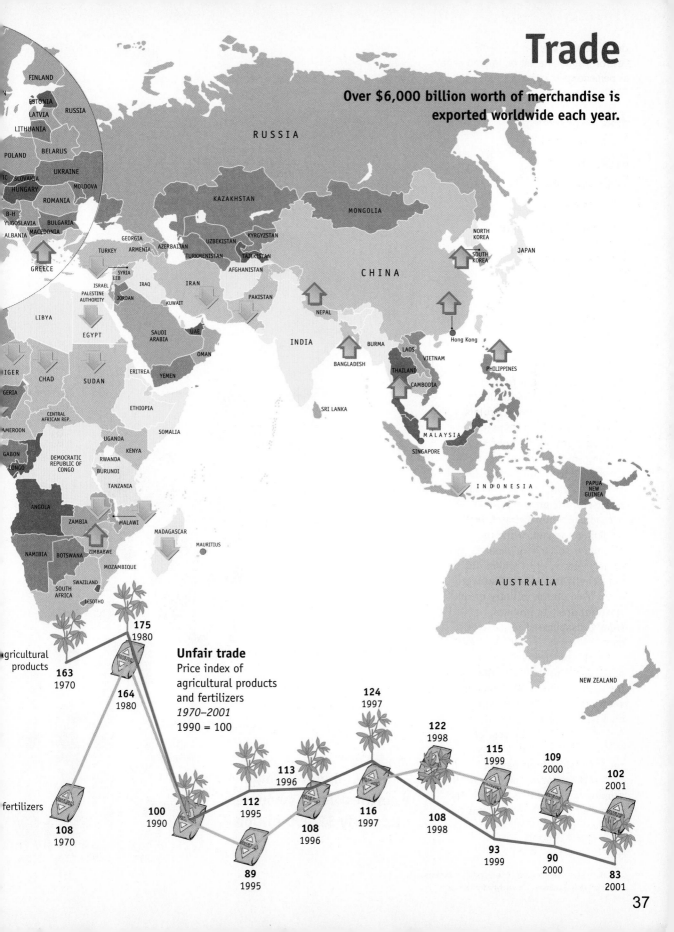

# Trade

**Over $6,000 billion worth of merchandise is exported worldwide each year.**

FINLAND

ESTONIA
LATVIA
LITHUANIA
RUSSIA

POLAND
BELARUS

SLOVAKIA
HUNGARY
UKRAINE
MOLDOVA

ROMANIA

B-H
YUGOSLAVIA
BULGARIA
ALBANIA MACEDONIA

GREECE

RUSSIA

KAZAKHSTAN

MONGOLIA

NORTH KOREA

JAPAN

GEORGIA
ARMENIA AZERBAIJAN
TURKEY

UZBEKISTAN KYRGYZSTAN
TURKMENISTAN TAJIKISTAN

SOUTH KOREA

SYRIA
LEB
IRAQ
ISRAEL
JORDAN
PALESTINE AUTHORITY

IRAN

AFGHANISTAN

KUWAIT

PAKISTAN

CHINA

LIBYA

EGYPT

SAUDI ARABIA

UAE

OMAN

NEPAL

Hong Kong

INDIA

BURMA

IGER
CHAD
SUDAN

ERITREA
YEMEN

BANGLADESH

LAOS
VIETNAM

THAILAND
CAMBODIA

PHILIPPINES

GERIA

CENTRAL AFRICAN REP.

ETHIOPIA

SRI LANKA

AMEROON

SOMALIA

MALAYSIA

GABON
CONGO

DEMOCRATIC REPUBLIC OF CONGO

UGANDA
RWANDA
BURUNDI

KENYA

SINGAPORE

TANZANIA

INDONESIA

PAPUA NEW GUINEA

ANGOLA
ZAMBIA
MALAWI

MADAGASCAR

MAURITIUS

NAMIBIA
BOTSWANA
ZIMBABWE

MOZAMBIQUE

AUSTRALIA

SWAZILAND
SOUTH AFRICA
LESOTHO

NEW ZEALAND

**175**
1980

agricultural
products

**163**
1970

**164**
1980

## Unfair trade
Price index of
agricultural products
and fertilizers
*1970–2001*
1990 = 100

**124**
1997

**122**
1998

**113**
1996

**115**
1999

**109**
2000

**102**
2001

fertilizers

**112**
1995

**100**
1990

**108**
1996

**116**
1997

**108**
1998

**108**
1970

**89**
1995

**93**
1999

**90**
2000

**83**
2001

## Debt servicing

Cost of paying interest on foreign debt as percentage of exports
*2000*

- 40% and over
- 20% – 39%
- 10% – 19%
- under 10%
- no data

## Overseas development aid received

as percentage of GDP
*2000*

- 20% and over
- 10% – 19%

Poor countries often find themselves saddled with debts taken on by their former rulers, forced to commit large parts of their earnings from exports to keeping up interest payments. Irresponsible lending in the late 1970s and early 1980s is as much a cause of the problem as irresponsible borrowing. But the lenders get repaid, while the borrowers suffer – or their subjects do, most of whom did not benefit from loans that were often used on the military or on wasteful prestige projects, or simply disappeared because of corruption.

The phrase "debt service" is particularly revealing of the way the system works. What this map shows is not the cost to poor countries of paying back their foreign debts, but the cost of simply "servicing" it, by paying the interest without paying back any of the capital. The debt itself remains a continuing burden. The only way to break the cycle is to forgive the debt.

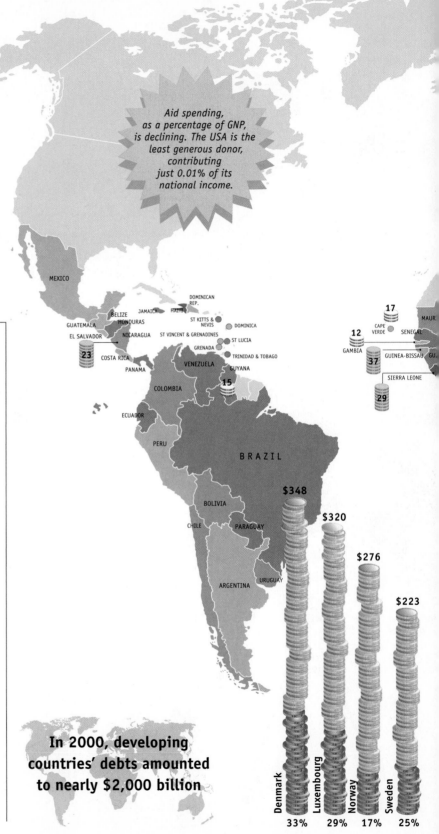

Aid spending, as a percentage of GNP, is declining. The USA is the least generous donor, contributing just 0.01% of its national income.

In 2000, developing countries' debts amounted to nearly $2,000 billion

| | | | | |
|---|---|---|---|---|
| $348 | $320 | $276 | $223 | |
| Denmark | Luxembourg | Norway | Sweden | |
| 33% | 29% | 17% | 25% | |

From *The Penguin State of the World Atlas* (ISBN 0142003182)
Copyright © Myriad Editions / www.MyriadEditions.com

# Debt and Aid

The poorer countries of the world pay out more in interest on their debts than they receive in economic aid, most of which takes the form of low-interest loans.

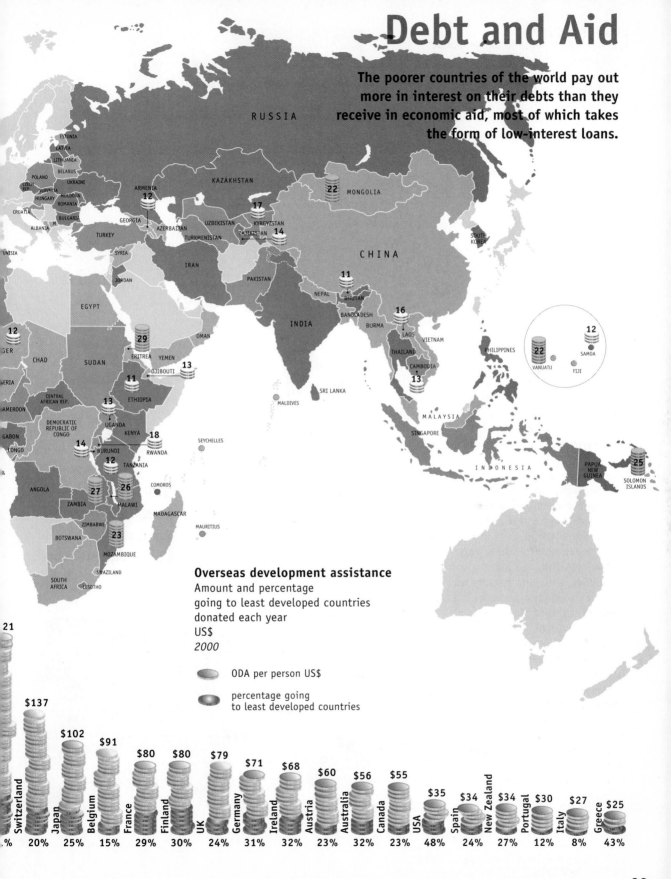

## Overseas development assistance
Amount and percentage
going to least developed countries
donated each year
US$
*2000*

ODA per person US$

percentage going
to least developed countries

## Greenhouse gases

Countries' shares of world carbon dioxide emissions
*2000*
countries emitting 0.1% or more of world total
World total: 22.7 billion tonnes a year

= 1%

= 0.1%

Annual emissions of $CO_2$ per person
*2000*
tonnes

15 and over

10.0 – 14.9

5.0 – 9.9

under 5

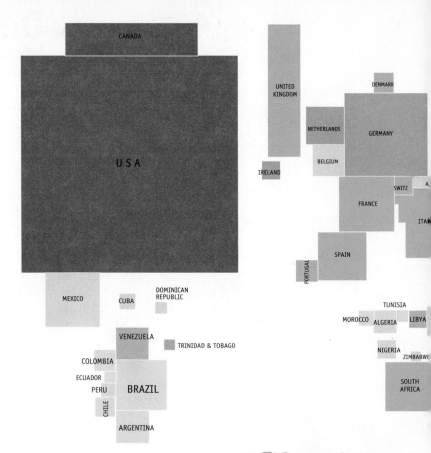

CANADA
UNITED KINGDOM
DENMARK
NETHERLANDS
GERMANY
IRELAND
BELGIUM
USA
SWITZ
A
FRANCE
ITA
PORTUGAL
SPAIN
MEXICO
CUBA
DOMINICAN REPUBLIC
TUNISIA
MOROCCO
ALGERIA
LIBYA
VENEZUELA
TRINIDAD & TOBAGO
NIGERIA
COLOMBIA
ZIMBABWE
ECUADOR
PERU
BRAZIL
SOUTH AFRICA
CHILE
ARGENTINA

Increasing energy use causes greater emissions of greenhouse gases – of which the most important is carbon dioxide ($CO_2$). The destruction of forests (see pages 36–37) means less $CO_2$ is absorbed by trees.

If the current increase in average temperatures continues, it will cause major climate change, reducing rainfall in some areas and increasing it in others. This will affect natural habitats worldwide, and will probably lead to the extinction of many species. There is also the risk of the Arctic and Antarctic ice caps melting, which would cause sea levels to rise, flooding small islands and low-lying coastal areas.

The fact that there have always been large temperature fluctuations over long time periods is used by some governments as an excuse for inaction.

## Global warming

Increase in average annual global temperature
*1991–2002*
compared with average for
*1961–1990*
degrees centigrade

**Every year, between 1991 and 2002, was warmer than the annual average for the previous 30 years**

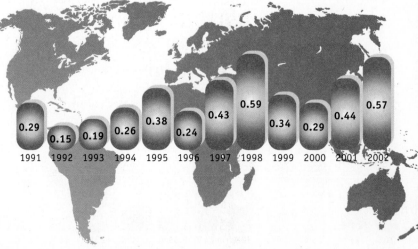

| 1991 | 1992 | 1993 | 1994 | 1995 | 1996 | 1997 | 1998 | 1999 | 2000 | 2001 | 2002 |
|------|------|------|------|------|------|------|------|------|------|------|------|
| 0.29 | 0.15 | 0.19 | 0.26 | 0.38 | 0.24 | 0.43 | 0.59 | 0.34 | 0.29 | 0.44 | 0.57 |

From *The Penguin State of the World Atlas* (ISBN 0142003182)
Copyright © Myriad Editions / www.MyriadEditions.com

# Climate Change

**World temperatures appear to be rising, but whether this is a result of the greenhouse effect remains controversial.**

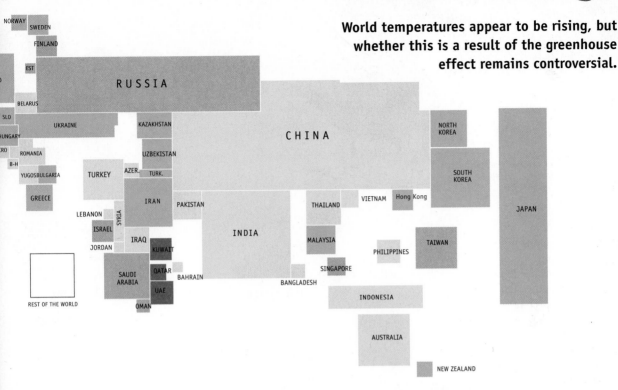

NORWAY
SWEDEN
FINLAND
EST
RUSSIA
BELARUS
SLO
UKRAINE
KAZAKHSTAN
HUNGARY
CRO
ROMANIA
B-H
YUGOSLAVIA BULGARIA
GREECE
TURKEY
AZER.
TURK.
UZBEKISTAN
IRAN
PAKISTAN
LEBANON
SYRIA
ISRAEL
JORDAN
IRAQ
KUWAIT
SAUDI ARABIA
QATAR
UAE
BAHRAIN
OMAN
CHINA
INDIA
THAILAND
VIETNAM
Hong Kong
MALAYSIA
SINGAPORE
BANGLADESH
PHILIPPINES
NORTH KOREA
SOUTH KOREA
JAPAN
TAIWAN
INDONESIA
AUSTRALIA
NEW ZEALAND
REST OF THE WORLD

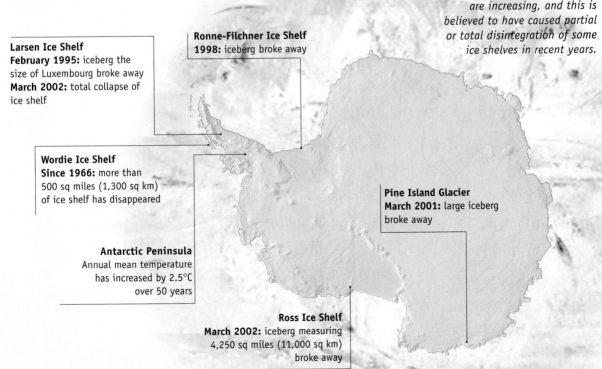

**The Antarctic**
*Average temperatures in parts of the Antarctic are increasing, and this is believed to have caused partial or total disintegration of some ice shelves in recent years.*

**Ronne-Filchner Ice Shelf**
**1998:** iceberg broke away

**Larsen Ice Shelf**
**February 1995:** iceberg the size of Luxembourg broke away
**March 2002:** total collapse of ice shelf

**Wordie Ice Shelf**
**Since 1966:** more than 500 sq miles (1,300 sq km) of ice shelf has disappeared

**Pine Island Glacier**
**March 2001:** large iceberg broke away

**Antarctic Peninsula**
Annual mean temperature has increased by 2.5°C over 50 years

**Ross Ice Shelf**
**March 2002:** iceberg measuring 4,250 sq miles (11,000 sq km) broke away

## People infected with HIV/AIDS

As percentage of total population
*end 2001*

- 15.0% and over
- 5.0% – 14.9%
- 1.0% – 4.9%
- 0.5% – 0.9%
- under 0.5%
- no data

**Highest infection rate:** Botswana 39%, Zimbabwe 34%, Swaziland 33%, Lesotho 31%

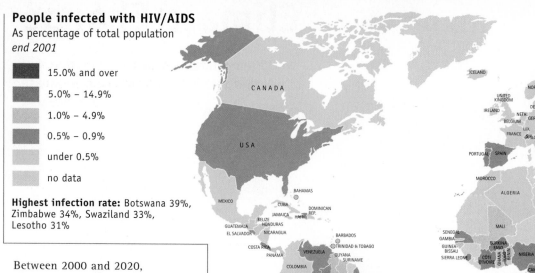

Between 2000 and 2020, 68 million people will die of HIV/AIDS, 55 million of them in Sub-Saharan Africa. These estimates, like all estimates of the epidemic, will probably be revised upwards as further information becomes available.

Infection rates for young people are two to three times faster among women than men. The human cost is huge; alongside the death count, there are other casualties of the epidemic – for example the 1.7 million AIDS orphans in southern Africa.

Ignorance, superstition, a refusal by too many governments to face the facts, and plain embarrassment combine to make it hard to respond to the crisis. Inhibitions about practicing and teaching safer sex are killing people.

### By 2020 more people will have died from HIV/AIDS than the total killed in both world wars

From *The Penguin State of the World Atlas* (ISBN 0142003182)
Copyright © Myriad Editions / www.MyriadEditions.com

### Eastern Europe and Central Asia

*Injecting drugs is causing rates of HIV to increase rapidly, especially among young people.*

**Russia:**
*up to 90% of infections are attributed to injecting drug use.*

**CIS:**
*almost 80% of registered new infections between 1997 and 2000 were in under-29-year-olds.*

**Uzbekistan:**
*during the first 6 months of 2002 as many new cases of HIV were recorded as the total for the preceding decade.*

### Food insecurity in the developing world

*HIV/AIDS contributes to food insecurity because it leads to:*
- *shortage of labor*
- *loss of wages*
- *disruption of the transfer of skills down generations*
- *additional financial burdens.*

### The unaffordable cost of treatment

*Drugs are available that prolong the life of a person infected by HIV/AIDS, but at prices that cannot be afforded by most people in developing countries.*

### Small signs of improvement

*Awareness campaigns, and prevention programs are beginning to reduce HIV rates among young women.*

**South Africa:**
*rate among pregnant women under 20 **down** from 21% in 1998 to 15.4% in 2001.*

**Uganda:**
*rate among pregnant women in urban areas **down** from 29.5% in 1992 to 11.25% in 2000.*

**Cambodia:**
*rate among sex workers **down** from 42% in 1998 to 29% in 2002.*

# HIV/AIDS

**Infection by HIV/AIDS can be prevented, but, so far, cannot be cured.**

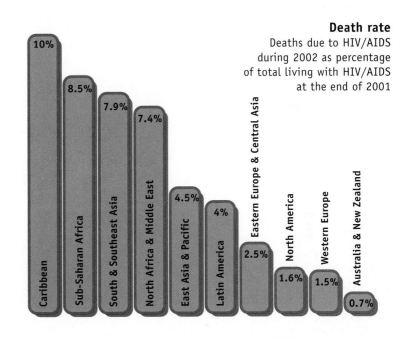

### Death rate
Deaths due to HIV/AIDS during 2002 as percentage of total living with HIV/AIDS at the end of 2001

- 10% Caribbean
- 8.5% Sub-Saharan Africa
- 7.9% South & Southeast Asia
- 7.4% North Africa & Middle East
- 4.5% East Asia & Pacific
- 4% Latin America
- 2.5% Eastern Europe & Central Asia
- 1.6% North America
- 1.5% Western Europe
- 0.7% Australia & New Zealand

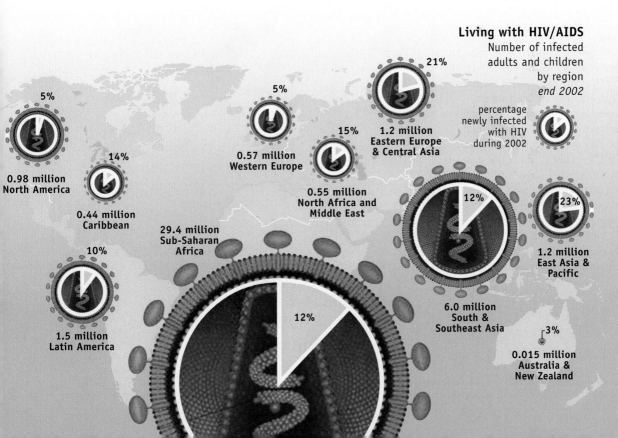

### Living with HIV/AIDS
Number of infected adults and children by region *end 2002*

*percentage newly infected with HIV during 2002*

- 5% — 0.98 million North America
- 14% — 0.44 million Caribbean
- 10% — 1.5 million Latin America
- 5% — 0.57 million Western Europe
- 15% — 0.55 million North Africa and Middle East
- 21% — 1.2 million Eastern Europe & Central Asia
- 12% — 29.4 million Sub-Saharan Africa
- 12% — 6.0 million South & Southeast Asia
- 23% — 1.2 million East Asia & Pacific
- 3% — 0.015 million Australia & New Zealand

SSIA

MONGOLIA

CHINA

SOUTH KOREA

JAPAN

EPAL

BHUTAN

BANGLADESH

LAOS

VIETNAM

THAILAND

CAMBODIA

Hong Kong

PHILIPPINES

SRI LANKA

MALAYSIA

SINGAPORE

INDONESIA

PAPUA NEW GUINEA

FIJI

AUSTRALIA

NEW ZEALAND

43

## Hungry children

Percentage of children under 5 years of age moderately or severely underweight
*2000*

| | |
|---|---|
| | over 40% |
| | 21% – 40% |
| | 11% – 20% |
| | 6% – 10% |
| | 1% – 5% |
| | no data |

### Undernourished adults

40% or more of population undernourished

Each year about 9 million people die from hunger-related diseases, and the health of 2 billion people is affected by a lack of vital nutrients in their food. Yet there is in principle enough food for all. Malnutrition in the poor world contrasts with over-nutrition in the rich world. The global food market shows particularly large surpluses of grain.

One marked improvement in world affairs over the past half century is that famines now occur almost solely as the side effect of war. But the capacity to transfer large amounts of food where necessary in an emergency has not translated into an efficient and fair system in normal times.

In the richer countries, a super-abundance of calories is as much of a problem as a lack of them. Poor diet is widespread in richer countries. Obesity is a serious health issue (see pages 118–19). Eating disorders such as anorexia and bulimia are also widespread.

**Two billion people – one third of the world's population – suffer from malnutrition**

From *The Penguin State of the World Atlas* (ISBN 0142003182)
Copyright © Myriad Editions / www.MyriadEditions.com

# Malnutrition

**There is enough food in the world to feed everybody. The problem lies in the distribution. Much is wasted while many starve.**

RUSSIA

KAZAKHSTAN

MONGOLIA

NORTH KOREA

CZECH REP.
UKRAINE
HUNGARY
MOLDOVA
ROMANIA
CROATIA B-H
YUG
M.
ALBANIA
GEORGIA
ARMENIA
AZERBAIJAN
UZBEKISTAN
KYRGYZSTAN
TURKEY

CHINA

TUNISIA
SYRIA
LEB
IRAQ
IRAN
AFGHANISTAN
PALESTINE AUTHORITY
JORDAN
KUWAIT
PAKISTAN

LIBYA
EGYPT
SAUDI ARABIA
BAHRAIN
QATAR
UAE
OMAN
NEPAL
BHUTAN
BANGLADESH
BURMA

GER
CHAD
SUDAN
ERITREA
YEMEN
DJIBOUTI
INDIA
LAOS
VIETNAM
THAILAND
CAMBODIA
PHILIPPINES

ERIA
CENTRAL AFRICAN REP.
ETHIOPIA
SOMALIA
SRI LANKA
MALDIVES

AMEROON
DEMOCRATIC REPUBLIC OF CONGO
UGANDA
KENYA
RWANDA
SEYCHELLES
MALAYSIA
SINGAPORE

CONGO
BURUNDI
TANZANIA
COMOROS
INDONESIA
PAPUA NEW GUINEA
SOLOMON ISLANDS

ANGOLA
ZAMBIA
MALAWI
MADAGASCAR
MAURITIUS
NAMIBIA
ZIMBABWE
BOTSWANA
MOZAMBIQUE
SWAZILAND
LESOTHO

KIRIBATI
VANUATU
FIJI

## Malnourished and vulnerable

Deaths from communicable diseases, maternal and perinatal conditions and nutritional deficiences, as a percentage of all deaths 2001

*Malnutrition due to shortage of calories or to a deficiency of vital minerals leaves people vulnerable to common infections such as measles and diarrhea. In turn, infections and intestinal parasites can reduce people's ability to absorb nutrients from their food.*

15% AMERICAS

71% AFRICA

6% EUROPE

43% EAST MEDITERRANEAN

40% SOUTH-EAST ASIA

15% WESTERN PACIFIC

From *The Penguin State of the World Atlas* (ISBN 0142003182)
Copyright © Myriad Editions / www.MyriadEditions.com

## Trading in narcotics

Major countries involved in
illicit narcotics trade
*2000 where known*

- production or transport of illicit narcotics
- supply of chemicals for production of illicit drugs
- $ financial institutions engage in currency transactions involving proceeds from international narcotics trafficking

### Major distribution routes

- cocaine
- heroin
- ecstasy

The market for illicit drugs is very small. Of countries for which estimates exist, it is only in Russia that over 1 percent of the adult population uses opiates, and only in the USA that over 2 percent uses cocaine. However, the selling price is so high that turnover and profit are huge.

The total value of the trade is unknown because it is illegal, and because street prices vary widely. A UN estimate is that the total value of the trade in illicit drugs is well over $400 billion a year.

Criminalization of some drugs does not restrict the trade – it just makes criminals out of the users. To pay for their addiction, many heroin users become sellers (creating new users in the process) and turn to petty crime and prostitution.

**The global trade in illegal drugs is worth twice as much as the motor vehicle industry**

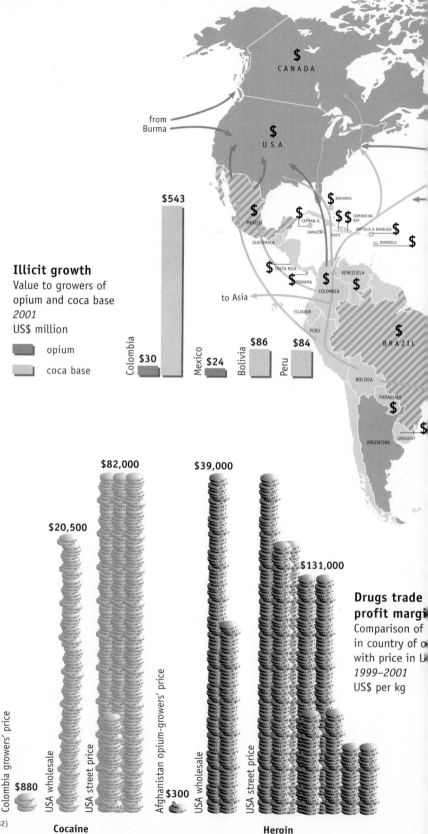

CANADA

from Burma

USA

$543

to Asia

$ BAHAMAS
$ CAYMAN IS.
$ $ DOMINICAN REP.
MEXICO
JAMAICA HAITI ANTIGUA & BARBUDA
GUATEMALA DOMINICA
$ COSTA RICA VENEZUELA
$ PANAMA COLOMBIA
ECUADOR
PERU BRAZIL
BOLIVIA
PARAGUAY
$ 
ARGENTINA URUGUAY

### Illicit growth

Value to growers of opium and coca base
*2001*
US$ million

- opium
- coca base

Colombia $543 / $30
Mexico $24
Bolivia $86
Peru $84

### Drugs trade profit margi

Comparison of
in country of o
with price in U
*1999–2001*
US$ per kg

**Cocaine**

- Colombia growers' price $880
- USA wholesale $20,500
- USA street price $82,000

**Heroin**

- Afghanistan opium-growers' price $300
- USA wholesale $39,000
- USA street price $131,000

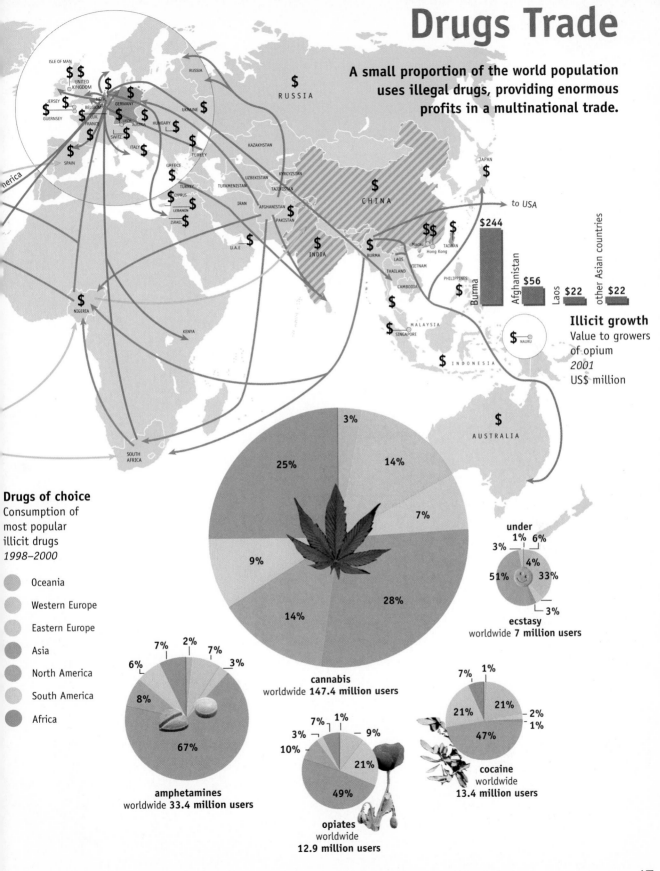

# Drugs Trade

A small proportion of the world population uses illegal drugs, providing enormous profits in a multinational trade.

to USA

**Illicit growth**
Value to growers
of opium
*2001*
US$ million

Burma $244
Afghanistan $56
Laos $22
other Asian countries $22

**Drugs of choice**
Consumption of
most popular
illicit drugs
*1998–2000*

- Oceania
- Western Europe
- Eastern Europe
- Asia
- North America
- South America
- Africa

**cannabis**
worldwide **147.4 million users**

3%
14%
7%
28%
14%
9%
25%

**ecstasy**
worldwide **7 million users**

under 1%
6%
3%
4%
33%
3%
51%

**amphetamines**
worldwide **33.4 million users**

2%
7%
7%
3%
6%
8%
67%

**opiates**
worldwide
**12.9 million users**

7% 1%
3%
10%
9%
21%
49%

**cocaine**
worldwide
**13.4 million users**

7% 1%
21%
21%
2%
1%
47%